WEIRD AND WONDERFUL
WILDLIFE

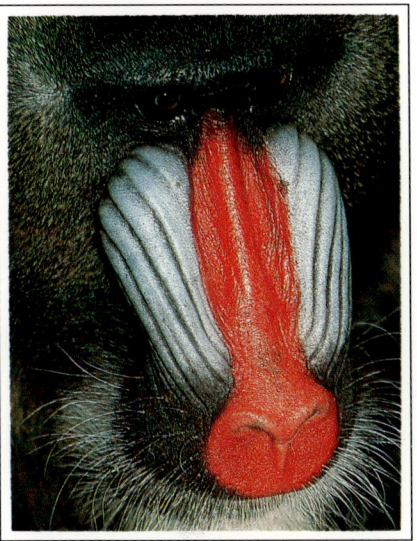

Chronicle Books · San Francisco

TOUCAN
Toco toucan

There are 37 species in the brilliant toucan family (*Ramphastidae*), all living in the tropical forests of South and Central America. This is the largest and brightest – features that allowed the humorist and talented bird painter Edward Lear to portray it despite his failing eyesight, though he complained that '. . . after this, no bird under an ostrich should I soon be able to see to do.'

The male sports a spectacular beak that can grow as long as 20 inches (50 cm). The beak is surprisingly light and is not used as a weapon, though toucans raid other nests and males clash bills together or peck at hollow logs for the sake of making a noise. The beak helps these heavy birds reach seeds on twigs too frail to offer them a perch. It is also used to groom other birds in the social groups to which toucans usually belong. These straggling flocks often make outings, yelping and croaking through the forest. They eat mainly seeds, fruit and small lizards, sometimes playfully tossing these items round the group from beak to beak.

ORANG-UTAN
Pongo pygmaeus

The name in Malaysian means 'man from the forest'; aptly, for unlike other 'great apes', orang-utans spend nearly all their time in the rainforest treetops of Borneo and Sumatra. The orang's face is framed with pouches of leathery skin and the thick epaulettes of hair on their shoulders act as a cape to shed the rain.

Orangs build loose nests in the trees in which to rear their young. Spidery creatures about the size of a kitten at birth, young orangs are totally dependent on their close-knit family unit for two or three years.

These gentle fruit- and leaf-eaters communicate in weird whoops and howls. They are full of curiosity and clever at manipulating objects with their hands – in zoos, they have a reputation for picking locks and separating everything in their cages into tiny pieces. Dwindling habitats and excessive hunting have reduced the wild orang population to around 5000 and attempts to reintroduce captive-bred animals are seldom successful because they prove too trusting in the wild after experiencing contact with humans.

RED-EYED LEAF FROG
Agalychnis callidryas

The natural world's greatest cataloguer, Carl Linnaeus, was no admirer of frogs: 'These foul and loathsome animals are,' he observed, 'abhorrent because of their cold body, pale colour, cartilaginous skeleton, filthy skin, fierce aspect, calculating eye, offensive smell, harsh voice, squalid habitation and terrible venom.'

These colourful and harmless little creatures prove him wrong on nearly every count. They live flattened against leaves high in tropical forests along the Caribbean coast of Costa Rica where their courtship is a high-wire act beginning with a face-to-face meeting along a twig. Then the female turns around and the male grasps her slippery body from behind in a tight embrace. More than once, with the male still attached, she clambers down to a pond, gathers water into her bladder, climbs back into the treetops to lay fertilized eggs in a cupped leaf, releasing water over them to prevent their drying out. When the tadpoles hatch they wriggle towards daylight, eventually launching themselves into mid air and – with luck – into the pond below.

MEERKAT
Suricta suricatta

The meerkat is a small southern African mongoose that lives in large colonies, often in association with other mongoose species or with ground squirrels. Though quite capable of digging their own burrows, meerkats prefer those dug by other animals. They like to bask in the sun at the burrow entrance or stand in a sociable line, chattering continuously.

Meerkat colonies forage as a team, with each individual taking turns to stand guard on a prominent tree stump or shrub while the others feed by scratching and digging for insects and spiders. If menaced by a hawk or other predator, meerkat groups bolt for cover on a whistled warning from the sentry currently on duty.

Easily tamed, meerkats are often kept as pets. Their lemur-like faces and beguiling poses belie impressive courage. They will fearlessly attack and eat giant desert scorpions that much larger animals will avoid, and groups of them have been known to chase off venomous snakes that threaten to prey on their young.

EMPEROR PENGUIN
Apterodytes forsteri

This is the largest and most glamorous of several dozen species of penguin, or *Apterodytes*, from the Greek words meaning 'wingless diver'. All penguins live in the Southern Hemisphere, most, including the Emperor, on the ice floes of Antarctica, but some (like the Galapagos Penguin) in warmer areas close to the equator. Sociable beings, penguins will always seek out company, if only to stand with each other in silence. Humans need only imitate their cry to attract a cluster of birds.

The initially corpulent male penguins fast throughout the period of courtship, mating and the nine weeks spent incubating an egg between their feet. In the absence of an egg, they have tried to hatch snowballs, stones, tin cans, cameras and even a researcher's fist. They shed nearly half their weight during this dark winter vigil, relieved only when, after feeding at sea, their mate returns to help rear the resulting chick.

Penguins have many foes, including seals and toothed whales, and competition from humans for the fish on which they feed is growing, yet the survival of these engaging birds seems assured for the present.

DUCK-BILLED PLATYPUS
Ornithorhynchus anatinus

This bizarre animal was first found on the Hawkesbury River in eastern Australia in 1797. Its discoverers thought they had found an aquatic mole with webbed feet and '. . . the upper and lower mandibles of a duck'. It immediately became a controversial beast and stayed that way for nearly a century. Was it a bird? A mammal? A missing link? Did it lay eggs?

A brisk trade in specimens developed; the first arriving in England in 1798 was widely thought to be a hoax. Two 'platypus eggs' shipped in a few years later proved to be tortoise eggs. In 1884, however, Cambridge zoologist W.H. Caldwell shot an *Ornithorhynchus* which had just laid one egg and had another still inside her. Further research showed that the platypus controls its body temperature and, though without nipples, has the mammary glands common to all mammals.

Much else about the platypus is unusual. Its bill, unlike that of a duck, is soft and sensitive. Thorny spurs on the animal's rear ankles are hollow and carry venom from glands in the thigh.

LEOPARD
Panthera pardus

One of the most adaptable of living mammals, leopards were once widespread from Africa to China. Today, they have been hunted virtually to extinction throughout most of North Africa and the Middle East and remain a threatened species in China.

The agility with which leopards climb and lodge their kill in trees allows them access to fenced-in livestock that are safe from most other animals, including lions. Deprived of their natural food and given the opportunity, they will also attack people. Unlike tigers, they kill at night and have broken into houses to do so. One British hunter, Major Jim Corbett, famous in northern India early this century, described '. . . two man-eating leopards that between them killed five hundred and twenty five human beings.' Observing their terrifying power he wrote, 'It is never safe to assume that a leopard is dead until it has been skinned.'

Attempts to lessen the demand for their fur have had some success, and in a few places leopards now flourish once more.

WALRUS
Odobenus rosmarus

The name walrus comes from Scandinavian words that mean 'whale horse'. When these bulky sea mammals move between their feeding grounds, they gather in herds that can number thousands. They are always gregarious and at breeding time a male will guard his 'harem'. They have a strong affection for their young and are very protective of each other; when one is wounded the whole herd joins in its defence.

Their powerful voices, sounding like something between a cow mooing and the deep baying of a mastiff, deter most intruders. But if they are attacked, their tusks, which appear after they are a year old and grow to a length of five feet (150 cm), make them formidable opponents. More often walruses use their tusks to dig in the shingle of the Arctic sea bed for shellfish. They eat these by grinding up the shells, swallowing only the soft parts.

Though in the past they have been hunted for food, ivory and oil, walruses are now protected everywhere and some populations are growing once again.

MONKEY-EATING EAGLE
(Philippines Eagle)

Pithecophaga jeffreyi

One of the two largest eagles in the world, these birds and the slightly larger South American Harpy are both members of the same harpy family.

Today their treetop world has shrunk and they live only on Mindanao Island in the Philippines. The notion of a bird eating a monkey was thought undesirable by President Marcos who renamed it the 'Philippines Eagle'. In fact, they seldom eat monkeys, but these rare birds are unique in their technique of snatching small mammals from the treetops in tropical forests, among them 'flying lemurs' (which are not proper lemurs and glide from branch to branch with the help of webbed arms).

By 1970 there were fewer than 100 Philippines Eagles left in the world, because animal dealers were plundering them for sale to zoos. In its native country it became a status symbol to own a stuffed specimen and local demand flourished. Besides this senseless killing, the eagles also suffered from man's destruction of their forest habitat. Despite strenuous conservation attempts, there are probably no more than 300 alive today.

POLAR BEAR
Ursus (Thalarctos) maritimus

'No stone, no bare spot in the snow, no dark shadow is black as a polar bear's nose. It is unmistakable miles away . . .' wrote Peary of a sight that has struck fear into many Arctic explorers. Solitary nomads for the most part, he-bears can weigh half-a-ton (500 kilograms) and tower twelve feet (3.6 metres) tall. Their dense fur even reaches under the soles of their feet and looks creamy-yellow against the dazzling Arctic snowscape.

In this hostile land, where injuries can prove fatal, wandering he-bears will often change course to duck a fight. During the mating season, however, several males are usually drawn to one she-bear and fight ferociously in single combat until all but one give up.

Polar bears are drawn to human settlements, scavenging garbage dumps or raiding food stores when they can. Where they become pests, wildlife rangers stun them with darts and airlift them to a safe distance. Fortunately these mighty carnivores are protected in law, or they would almost certainly have been exterminated by hunters.

JELLYFISH
Chysaora hyoscella

Jellyfish like this one lead a bizarre sex life: masculine at birth, they become simultaneously male and female, each capable of producing offspring, and they end their lives as females.

All jellyfish have a rudimentary nervous system; they are among the lowest animals to be made up of different sorts of cells. Some, like this one, have specialized cells that make them give off a luminous glow when disturbed. Others, like the lethal 'box jellies' whose victims are said to 'scream out in terrible agony and become irrational', can each have as many as 40 million stinging cells and are capable of killing a man in minutes.

In Australia, where jellyfish feed in shallow water along the Queensland coast, more swimmers have been killed by these deadly creatures than by sharks. Fortunately, people rarely swim in Arctic waters where the massive Lion's Mane jellyfish engulf large fish with their 130-ft (40-metre) long brown tentacles.

YELLOW BABOON
Papio cynocephalus

These most sociable of monkeys forage across the African savannah in troops that can number more than a hundred. Their well-organized bands have a vanguard of young males to protect the females who may have vulnerable young offspring clinging to their fur.

Baboons have a wide vocabulary and their warning bark often acts as an alarm for other animals such as the antelopes whose grazing land they share. Leopards are the baboon's chief enemies, sometimes snatching a young one from the fringe of a troop. A large male baboon, however, can turn the tables and kill its predator. Besides being dangerous, these monkeys are notorious thieves. Once, in South Africa, baboons stole a baby girl from her mother's care and killed her with bites to her head. Baboons can also be surprisingly protective: in South West Africa tamed baboons have been used to herd goats; one such animal would even gather straying kids and return them to their own mothers.

Rocky Mountain Goat
Oreamnos americanus

These animals are not really goats at all. They do not share the primitive Asian ancestor believed common to all true goats and sheep and are more closely related to the Alpine Chamois.

They inhabit a harsh glacial wilderness above the tree line, living in what the painter and naturalist John James Audubon called 'majestic solitude'. Bold and relaxed climbers, they make steady progress over the steep terrain high in the Rocky Mountains. In winter their hooves and muzzles turn black and are often all that can be seen of them against the snow and rock.

They have few enemies besides hunters with rifles, although in the mountains one is occasionally killed by an eagle. When they descend into the valleys, grizzly bears, wolves and coyotes attack them, but even grizzlies do not always manage to evade their powerful horns.

MALAGASY CHAMELEON
Chamaeleo pardalis

Like most other chameleons, this large species from the arid eastern side of Madagascar can adapt the colour and pattern of its skin to improve its camouflage in the trees where it hunts for insects and is preyed upon by snakes. Colour changes are probably controlled by the chameleon's nervous system and triggered by light changes as well as sounds or movements that cause alarm. The concentrations of specialized yellow, black and reflecting white cells in the skin adjust to vary the overall hue.

The chameleon moves slowly round the branches of trees during the day, and when it gets near enough to an insect or spider, it wraps its tail firmly around a twig to anchor itself and suddenly shoots out its tongue, which stretches almost the length of its own body. The round end of the tongue is gathered like a rolled-up sleeve around a long 'launching bone' on the reptile's lower jaw.

Tribal lore in parts of Madagascar and Africa labels the chameleon as a creature of the devil, to be feared and left unharmed.

GIANT PANDA
Ailuropus melanoleucus

Known locally as *Daxiongmao*, meaning 'large bear-cat', these solitary creatures live in mountainous southwestern China. They like the cool foggy air of the bamboo forests along the Tibetan highlands. They eat only bamboo and digest it so inefficiently that they are compelled to spend 14 hours every day on the ground feeding in order to survive.

The ancient Chinese believed pandas ate iron and copper and thrived only in times of peace when these were not in demand for weapons. Gifts of live pandas have long been a treasured symbol of goodwill – one was given to the Emperor of Japan as early as AD 685, and since then many distinguished statesmen around the world have been presented with pandas.

The first live panda arrived in the West in 1936. Although only 49 have been seen outside China, they have become a symbol for endangered wildlife. Now fewer than a thousand pandas survive in a dozen isolated groups. As they rarely breed in captivity, only immense effort and good fortune will save them from total extinction.

First published in the United States in 1991
by Chronicle Books

Conceived, edited and designed by Russell Ash & Bernard Higton
Copyright © 1991 by Russell Ash & Bernard Higton
Text by Robert Lamb and Bill Forse

Printed in Hong Kong by Imago

ISBN 0-87701-896-0

10 9 8 7 6 5 4 3 2 1

Chronicle Books
275 Fifth Street
San Francisco, CA
94103

Photo credits: Mandrill – Michael Dick/Animals Animals/Oxford Scientific Films (hereafter credited as OSF); Toucan – Hans Reinhard/Okapia/OSF; Orang-Utan – ZEFA; Red-eyed Leaf Frog – Michael Fogden/OSF; Meerkat – David Macdonald/OSF; Emperor Penguin – Doug Allan/OSF; Duck-billed Platypus – Jean-Philippe Varin/Jacana; Leopard – D. Woods/ZEFA; Walrus – C. Krebs/ZEFA; Monkey-eating Eagle – Brian J. Coates/Bruce Coleman Ltd; Polar Bear – Tom Ulrich/OSF; Jellyfish – Kathie Atkinson/OSF; Yellow Baboon – Stan Osolinski/OSF; Rocky Mountain Goat – Wendy Shattil & Bob Rozinski/OSF; Malagasy Chameleon – John Gerlach/Animals Animals/OSF; Giant Panda – Ralph A. Reinhold/Animals Animals/OSF.